A Writer's Resource

A Handbook for Writing and Research

Third Edition

Elaine P. Maimon
Governors State University

Janice H. Peritz
Queens College,
City University of New York

Kathleen Blake Yancey
Florida State University

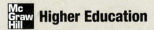 **Higher Education**

Boston   Burr Ridge, IL   Dubuque, IA   New York   San Francisco   St. Louis
Bangkok   Bogotá   Caracas   Kuala Lumpur   Lisbon   London   Madrid   Mexico City
Milan   Montreal   New Delhi   Santiago   Seoul   Singapore   Sydney   Taipei   Toronto

Higher Education

Published by McGraw-Hill, an imprint of The McGraw-Hill Companies, Inc., 1221 Avenue of the Americas, New York, NY 10020. Copyright © 2010, 2007, 2003. All rights reserved. No part of this publication may be reproduced or distributed in any form or by any means, or stored in a database or retrieval system, without the prior written consent of The McGraw-Hill Companies, Inc., including but not limited to, in any network or other electronic storage or transmission, or broadcast for distance learning.

1 2 3 4 5 6 7 8 9 0 DOW DOC 0 9

Comb: ISBN: 978-0-07-736746-6   Spiral: ISBN: 978-0-07-736879-1
         MHID: 0-07-736746-4   MHID: 0-07-736879-7

Vice President and Editor in Chief: *Michael Ryan*
Publisher: *David S. Patterson*
Senior Sponsoring Editor: *Christopher Bennem*
Director of Development: *Dawn Groundwater*
Development Editor: *Anne Kemper*
Executive Marketing Manager: *Allison Jones*
Market Development Manager: *Molly Meneely*
Lead Production Editor: *Brett Coker*

Manuscript Editor: *Margaret Moore*
Lead Designer: *Cassandra Chu*
Interior and Cover Designer: *Maureen McCutcheon*
Art and Photo Editor: *Sonia Brown*
Production Supervisors: *Randy Hurst, Richard DeVitto*
Lead Media Project Manager: *Ron Nelms*
Composition: *9/11 New Century Schoolbook by Thompson Type*
Printing: *45# Pub Matte Thinbulk by R.R. Donnelley & Sons*

Cover images: (*from left to right*) © *Philadelphia Museum of Art/CORBIS;* © *NASA/Roger Ressmeyer/CORBIS; Nevros/Folio, Inc.;* © *Jon Hicks/CORBIS*

Credits: *The credits section for this book begins on page C-1 and is considered an extension of the copyright page.*

Library of Congress Cataloging-in-Publication Data
Maimon, Elaine P.
  A writer's resource: a handbook for writing and research APA Update / Elaine P. Maimon, Janice H. Peritz, Kathleen Blake Yancey.—3rd ed.
    p. cm.
  Includes bibliographical references and indexes.
  ISBN-13: 978-0-07-338377-4   ISBN-13: 978-0-07-736746-6 (alk. paper)
  ISBN-10: 0-07-338377-5   ISBN-10: 0-07-736746-4 (alk. paper)
  1. English language—Rhetoric—Handbooks, manuals, etc. 2. English language—Grammar—Handbooks, manuals, etc. 3. Report writing—Handbooks, manuals, etc. I. Peritz, Janice. II. Yancey, Kathleen Blake, 1950– III. Title.

PE1408.M3366 2009
808'.042—dc22   2008047101

The Internet addresses listed in the text were accurate at the time of publication. The inclusion of a Web site does not indicate an endorsement by the authors or McGraw-Hill, and McGraw-Hill does not guarantee the accuracy of the information presented at these sites.

This reprint contains the 2009 APA updates.

Catalyst 2.0

The Online Learning Center for *A Writer's Resource,* Third Edition (http://www.mhhe.com/awr3) provides full coverage of writing, researching, and editing, featuring diagnostic quizzes that help students assess their knowledge of usage, grammar, punctuation, mechanics, and spelling. A list of print and online resources in 30 disciplines provides a starting point for student research projects. "How to Use This Book" tutorials teach students to locate information in the textbook with ease.

The site features all the resources of Catalyst 2.0, the premiere online tool for writing, research, and editing.

To access premium Catalyst content, please go to the Online Learning Center for *A Writer's Resource* Third Edition at http://www.mhhe.com/awr3 and click on the "Enter Catalyst 2.0" graphic shown below in the middle of the home page.

Catalyst 2.0 features interactive tutorials on document design and visual rhetoric, guides for avoiding plagiarism and evaluating sources, electronic writing tutors for composing a range of essays, and more than 4,500 exercises with feedback in grammar, usage, and punctuation.

Preface

As we wrote the first edition of *A Writer's Resource,* our students were always on our minds. We knew that today's students' perspectives on college life were different from those of previous generations of students, and so were their expectations. Most college students today have never known a world without the Internet. Advances in technologies ensure that they are constantly connected to a wealth of information on almost any topic, as well as to one another. Raised on the Web, television, and advertising, they are highly attuned to visual images. At the same time, students with careers and families are entering, and reentering, academia with their own rich set of experiences and expectations. More than ever before, today's students represent an abundance of linguistic and cultural backgrounds, needing a variety of approaches to writing and editing at the college level. Multitasking at unprecedented levels, they need a handbook they can rely on in all their courses: whether that means learning about revision in their English composition class, preparing PowerPoints for a speech course, or looking for help with integrating sources into a history assignment.

Students are different,

the tools are different,

but the goals are the same:

writing well and succeeding in college and beyond.

As students change, so, too, do the tools that students use for writing and research. Research occurs online via databases and the Web, and the greatest challenges students face are not in finding sources, but in choosing and evaluating the most appropriate sources and using them effectively in their projects. Word processing and presentation software and writing for the Web have increased the importance of visuals and design in writing. Many composition courses make use of digital technologies such as electronic portfolios or blogs and use Blackboard or other course-management systems to foster student collaboration and online peer review.

Even though the occasions, tools, and audiences for writing seem more varied than ever, the fundamental goals of composition courses persist. Instructors strive to produce students who can think critically, recognize rhetorical situations, communicate clearly and effectively, write in a variety of genres, and edit their own work. Students must be discerning and ethical researchers, acknowledging the contributions of others and documenting sources appropriately. And composition courses still aim to build writing skills that students will carry with them into their other courses, their work in the community, and their professional lives. In response to these goals—suggested by the Writing Program Administrators Outcomes Statement for First-Year Composition (reproduced on p. xiv) and those of many colleges and universities—*A Writer's Resource* pays new attention to commonly identified outcomes for composition to help students track their progress and understand how they may be assessed.

Today's students need a handbook with state-of-the-art, accessible resources on writing, researching, editing, and design—a handbook they can rely on for all their academic writing.

In revising this text, we have dedicated ourselves to making *A Writer's Resource* an even stronger, more current, and more versatile resource for achieving excellence in the ever-changing environments that students encounter in college.

Features of *A Writer's Resource*

Specific, student- and instructor-tested features of *A Writer's Resource* equip today's students with tools for learning, writing, researching, and editing. The book also provides students and teachers with access to powerful online resources.

A Ready Resource

The third edition of *A Writer's Resource* meets the needs of busy students with new, quickly accessible features that make it an even more convenient reference tool.

New Resources for Writers: Identifying and Editing Common Problems foldout

This handy reference presents easy access to fixes for the most common errors students make when editing for clarity, grammatical conventions, and correctness (punctuation, mechanics, and spelling). On the back of this foldout, students will find **Quick Reference for Multilingual Writers,** a chart offering help with the most common problems that affect Generation 1.5 students and English language learners alike.

Revised and Expanded Resources for Writers foldouts for documenting in MLA and APA style

These foldouts reflect the most recent changes to these two styles of citation. On the front of each foldout, **Identifying and Documenting Sources,** flowcharts help guide students to the correct model citations in the text. On the reverse side, each panel includes visual guidelines for citing sources, showing where students can find the bibliographic information for a book, periodical, Web site, selection from an online database (MLA), or online article with Digital Object Identifier (APA). On the back of each foldout, flowcharts help guide students to the correct model citations in the text.

New Resources for Writers: Discipline-Specific Resources and World Map foldout

Since research forms a vital part of college writing, this pullout section includes up-to-date information on reference works and resources from a variety of disciplines. More reliable than a Google search, this listing of academically vetted sources provides students with a quick-reference guide to the places online and in the library where the research might reasonably start. A revised, full-color map of the world is found on the back of the foldout.

New attention to key writing outcomes

Writing Outcomes boxes at the beginning of each section indicate where students can find key material that will help them master aspects of writing such as rhetorical knowledge, the writing process, and critical thinking. Based on the WPA Outcomes Statement for First-Year Composition (reproduced on p. xiv), this feature helps students find the support they need to address the key issues in their writing on which they are likely to be assessed.

New checklists for self-assessment

These checklists on topics such as editing for style and avoiding plagiarism help students evaluate their work and reflect on processes for improving their writing.

New online interactive tutorials

The handbook offers important guidance for students throughout their college career and beyond, and these online guides help students get the most out of this valuable resource. Brief visual overviews to using the text accompany interactive quizzes that help students become more familiar with the text.

A Resource for Writing

A Writer's Resource recognizes the importance of critical thinking and academic writing in first-year composition.

Guidelines for the most common college writing assignments

Tab 3: Common Assignments across the Curriculum gives students step-by-step advice on writing the three most commonly assigned types of papers (informative, interpretive, and argumentative essays), as well as guidance on other common assignments including personal essays, case studies, lab reports, in-class essay exams, oral presentations with PowerPoint, and multimedia assignments. Three full student papers appear in this section as models.

A focus on critical thinking and effective writing across the curriculum

Although instructors in various disciplines may approach subject matter differently, thinking critically and writing logically are underlying expectations across the curriculum. For this reason, Tab 2: Writing and Designing Texts begins with a chapter on the connections among critical reading, thinking, and writing.

Real student writing

Because students learn best from models that relate to their actual experience, *A Writer's Resource* provides plentiful samples of student and professional writing for a variety of purposes—to inform, interpret, and argue. The chapter on revising presents a full-length edited student essay; the document design chapter contains a student's reflective essay from an electronic portfolio; the common assignments chapters include three student papers; and the MLA and APA documentation chapters each feature a complete student research report.

This edition includes three *new* student sample papers:

- Reflective essay from an electronic portfolio
- Informative report in the social sciences
- Argument paper

New expanded coverage of argument and visual argument

The third edition further equips students for success in this important genre, with fuller treatment of the classical appeals, fallacies, counterarguments, and the classical, Toulmin, and Rogerian structures of argument. New material in Chapter 4: Reading, Thinking, Writing: The Critical Connection and Chapter 11: Arguments invites students to recognize the persuasive messages that surround them and help them to use those techniques in their own arguments.

New visual rhetoric icon complements integrated coverage of visual rhetoric

This image appears throughout the text and in the table of contents on the tabs. It guides students and instructors to sections dealing with the use of visuals—a complete listing also appears in the Quick Guide to Key Resources at the back of the book. *A Writer's Resource* includes a chapter on Learning in a Multimedia World in Tab 1: Learning across the Curriculum and a chapter on Finding and Creating Effective Visuals in Tab 5: Researching. Coverage is also integrated throughout the text, particularly in Tab 2: Writing and Designing Texts. In addition, the book itself includes visuals drawn from various disciplines, time periods, and cultures.

New updated coverage of today's technologies

Today's student has more opportunities to write than ever before, including Facebook and MySpace pages, e-mail and texting, chat rooms, and blogs. The text gives advice on using online tools for learning; practical suggestions for using online resources to collaborate and revise; a chapter on designing papers and preparing print and online portfolios; advice for writing scannable résumés; and TextConnex boxes with advice on technology and useful links throughout the text.

Preparation for writing at work and in the community

Tab 4: Writing beyond College demonstrates how writing in college prepares students for success in the professional world. Special topics include applying for internships, producing résumés, service learning, and creating brochures and newsletters. In addition, Writing beyond College boxes throughout the book illustrate the variety of writing situations students are likely to encounter outside of college.

A Resource for Researching

A Writer's Resource helps students navigate the complexities of research today.

New updated and expanded coverage of MLA, APA, and CSE documentation

Tabs 6–8 now conform to the seventh edition of the *MLA Handbook for Writers of Research Papers* (2009), the sixth edition of the *Publication Manual of the American Psychological Association* (2010), and the seventh edition of the *CSE Manual for Authors, Editors, and Publishers* (2006). The text also includes up-to-date coverage of *Chicago Manual of Style* documentation. This expanded section contains 120 MLA citation models and 68 APA citation models.

New chapter on plagiarism, copyright, and intellectual property

Chapter 23: Plagiarism, Copyright, and Intellectual Property provides an overview of the issues of copyright, plagiarism, and fair use.

New expanded sections on integrating sources

In Chapter 24, more examples and guidelines give students additional advice on using sources effectively in their papers. More thorough explanation of acceptable and unacceptable paraphrases, summaries, and quotations enables students to avoid accidental plagiarism. An expanded overview of copyright, plagiarism, and fair use appears in Chapter 20: Plagiarism, Copyright, and Intellectual Property.

New Source Smart boxes

Appearing throughout Tab 5: Researching, these boxes offer students tips on researching wisely. Topics include creating a research strategy, conducting interviews, avoiding plagiarism, and integrating sources via summary, paraphrase, and quotation.

New expanded sections on how to evaluate and use online sources appropriately

Chapter 21 now includes an examination of the reliability of three Web sites. These guidelines help students conduct Web research wisely and choose sources appropriately. Chapter 24 helps students draw on a full range of media in their writing, with examples that include blog entries and audio podcasts.

New discussion of annotated bibliography

Chapter 24 includes a sample annotated bibliography. It shows students how to complete this common research assignment, enabling them to assess and track their sources.

A unique chapter on finding and creating effective visuals
Chapter 20: Finding and Creating Effective Visuals includes discussions of why and when students should—or should not—use images to reinforce a point and gives them practical advice on displaying information visually.

A Resource for Editing

A Writer's Resource helps today's students see how grammar fits into the writing process, so they can learn to become effective editors of their work.

Grammar in the context of editing
Most of the chapters in Tabs 9–11, which cover the conventions of English grammar, usage, punctuation, and mechanics, are structured first to teach students to identify a particular problem and then to edit to eliminate the problem in a way that strengthens their writing.

Identify and Edit boxes
These boxes appear in key style, grammar, and punctuation chapters. They give students (especially visual learners) strategies for identifying their most serious sentence problems and are especially useful for quick reference.

***New* common issues icon ✓**
This new icon appears throughout the text and in the table of contents, highlighting sections that discuss students' most common difficulties with grammar, style, word choice, punctuation, and mechanics. These sections are listed in the Quick Guide to Key Resources at the back of the book and referenced, for quick consultation, on the Resources for Writers: Identifying and Editing Common Problems foldout.

***New* interactive online Test Yourself diagnostic quizzes**
These interactive online diagnostics provide immediate feedback to students to let them know where they need improvement and where to find help in those areas. They help students gauge their strengths and weaknesses on the conventions of MLA and APA documentation, grammar, style, punctuation, and mechanics.

Advice on using grammar and style checkers
Boxes appearing near the beginning of most chapters in Tabs 9–11 warn students of the pitfalls of relying too much on computer grammar and style checkers when editing their work, empowering students to become their own grammar checkers.

A Resource for Learning

A Writer's Resource is unique in the amount of support it provides students to help them meet the challenges of learning in college.

A guide for success in college through writing

Tab 1: Learning across the Curriculum introduces students to the new territory of college and to college writing. In this unique section, we define concepts such as *discipline* and explain how to use writing as a tool for learning. New tips in Chapter 1 help students set priorities, take notes, and succeed in all their courses.

Abundant resources for multilingual writers

Starting in the very first tab, *A Writer's Resource* offers non-native speakers of English support for learning and writing in college. Chapter 3 advises multilingual students on how to use writing to deal with their unique challenges. Numerous For Multilingual Students boxes throughout the book and Tips for Multilingual Writers in Tab 12 (prepared by Maria Zlateva, director of ESL at Boston University) provide targeted advice on every stage of the writing process. A separate index for multilingual writers follows the main index. A complete list of all the For Multilingual Students boxes also appears in the back of the book. The Quick Reference for Multilingual Writers foldout offers handy grammar tips in a convenient format.

New attention to Generation 1.5 of English language learners

Chapter 3: Learning in a Multilingual World now addresses both traditional ESL students and members of Generation 1.5, who have marginal proficiency in English as well as one or more other languages.

Further resources for learning

The innovative final section of the book (Tab 13: Further Resources for Learning) provides students with a variety of resources—a timeline of world history, a glossary of selected terms from across the curriculum, a pullout map of the world, and a directory of print and online discipline-specific resources—that will come in handy for students in a wide variety of courses.

Charting the Territory boxes

These boxes provide students with examples of how requirements and conventions vary across the curriculum. They present relevant information on such topics as interpretive assignments in different disciplines and the function of the passive voice in scientific writing.

A Resource for Technology

Online Learning Center (www.mhhe.com/awr3)

Throughout *A Writer's Resource,* Web references in the margin let students know where they can find additional resources on the text's comprehensive Web site. Access to the site—which is powered by *Catalyst 2.0,* the premier online resource for writing, research, and editing—is free with every copy of *A Writer's Resource.* The site includes the following resources for students:

- Interactive tutorials on document design and visual rhetoric
- Guides for avoiding plagiarism and evaluating sources
- Electronic writing tutors for composing informative, interpretive, and argumentative papers
- Over 4,500 exercises with feedback in grammar, usage, and punctuation

Additional options online:

Connect Composition for *A Writer's Resource*
This online premium companion to the text provides students and instructors with:

- **Interactive exercises and assignments keyed to the chapters of the text** allow students to practice the material in the text and submit assignments online.
- **Digital diagnostics and study plan** allow students to test themselves and find where they might need help; Connect Composition will then suggest a course of study including video instruction, practice exercises, and a post-test.
- **Online peer review tools** allow instructors to administer peer review in a flexible, easy-to-use electronic format that helps students throughout the process of inventing, drafting, and revising their work.
- **Live, online tutors** via Net Tutor offer students help with their writing when instructors or writing centers might not be available.
- **Numerous additional interactive resources for writing and research,** including interactive writing tutors and tutorials for visual rhetoric and avoiding plagiarism, provide students with help throughout the writing process.

Connect Composition Plus: *The McGraw-Hill Handbook Online*
This interactive, economic alternative to the print text includes all of the features contained in Connect Composition *plus:*

- **All the content of the full handbook online,** optimized for online reading—with material broken out in easy-to-read chunks of information, with interactive elements integrated contextually throughout.
- **A state-of-the-art search portal** which allows students to explore the whole text using numerous digital navigational tools including text and advanced text search options, hyperlinked indexes and table of contents, interactive resources for writers pages for help with the most common problems, and

multimedia quick links that offer instant access to all of the
text's multimedia instruction in one place.

- **Over 100 Ask the Author video segments** integrated
throughout the digital text, providing students with instant
access multimedia guidance on the most commonly asked
questions about writing, researching, editing, and designing
their work.

- **An economical price** providing students access to the interactive text for approximately half the price of the print text.

CourseSmart is a new way for faculty to find and review eTextbooks. It
is also a great option for students who are interested in accessing their
course materials digitally and saving money. CourseSmart offers thou-
sands of the most commonly adopted textbooks across hundreds of courses
from a wide variety of higher education publishers. It is the only place for
faculty to review and compare the full text of a textbook online, providing
immediate access without the environmental impact of requesting a print
exam copy. At CourseSmart, students can save up to 50% off the cost of a
print book, reduce their impact on the environment, and gain access to
powerful web tools for learning including full text search, notes and highlighting, and e-mail tools for sharing notes between classmates.

McGraw Hill Tegrity campus

Tegrity Campus is a service that makes class time available all the
time by automatically capturing every lecture in a searchable format
for students to review when they study and complete assignments.
With a simple one-click start and stop process, you capture all computer screens and corresponding audio. Students replay any part of
any class with easy-to-use browser-based viewing on a PC or Mac.

Educators know that the more students can see, hear, and experience class resources, the better they learn. With Tegrity Campus, students quickly recall key moments by using Tegrity Campus's unique
search feature. This search helps students efficiently find what they
need, when they need it across an entire semester of class recordings.
Help turn all your students' study time into learning moments imme-
diately supported by your lecture.

To learn more about Tegrity, watch a two-minute Flash demo at
http://tegritycampus.mhhe.com.

WPA Outcomes Statement for First-Year Composition

Adopted by the Council of Writing Program Administrators (WPA), April 2000. For further information about the development of the Outcomes Statement, please see http://comppile .tamucc.edu/ WPAoutcomes/continue.html

For further information about the Council of Writing Program Administrators, please see http://www.wpacouncil.org

A version of this statement was published in WPA: Writing Program Administration 23.1/2 (fall/winter 1999): 59–66

Introduction

This statement describes the common knowledge, skills, and attitudes sought by first-year composition programs in American postsecondary education. To some extent, we seek to regularize what can be expected to be taught in first-year composition; to this end the document is not merely a compilation or summary of what currently takes place. Rather, the following statement articulates what composition teachers nationwide have learned from practice, research, and theory. This document intentionally defines only "outcomes," or types of results, and not "standards," or precise levels of achievement. The setting of standards should be left to specific institutions or specific groups of institutions.

Learning to write is a complex process, both individual and social, that takes place over time with continued practice and informed guidance. Therefore, it is important that teachers, administrators, and a concerned public do not imagine that these outcomes can be taught in reduced or simple ways. Helping students demonstrate these outcomes requires expert understanding of how students actually learn to write. For this reason we expect the primary audience for this document to be well-prepared college writing teachers and college writing program administrators. In some places, we have chosen to write in their professional language. Among such readers, terms such as "rhetorical" and "genre" convey a rich meaning that is not easily simplified. While we have also aimed at writing a document that the general public can understand, in limited cases we have aimed first at communicating effectively with expert writing teachers and writing program administrators.

These statements describe only what we expect to find at the end of first-year composition, at most schools a required general education course or sequence of courses. As writers move beyond first-year composition, their writing abilities do not merely improve. Rather, students' abilities not only diversify along disciplinary and professional lines but also move into whole new levels where expected outcomes expand, multiply, and diverge. For this reason, each statement of outcomes for first-year composition is followed by suggestions for further work that builds on these outcomes.

Rhetorical Knowledge

By the end of first-year composition, students should
- Focus on a purpose
- Respond to the needs of different audiences

- Respond appropriately to different kinds of rhetorical situations
- Use conventions of format and structure appropriate to the rhetorical situation
- Adopt appropriate voice, tone, and level of formality
- Understand how genres shape reading and writing
- Write in several genres

Faculty in all programs and departments can build on this preparation by helping students learn

- The main features of writing in their fields
- The main uses of writing in their fields
- The expectations of readers in their fields

Critical Thinking, Reading, and Writing

By the end of first-year composition, students should

- Use writing and reading for inquiry, learning, thinking, and communicating
- Understand a writing assignment as a series of tasks, including finding, evaluating, analyzing, and synthesizing appropriate primary and secondary sources
- Integrate their own ideas with those of others
- Understand the relationships among language, knowledge, and power

Faculty in all programs and departments can build on this preparation by helping students learn

- The uses of writing as a critical thinking method
- The interactions among critical thinking, critical reading, and writing
- The relationships among language, knowledge, and power in their fields

Processes

By the end of first-year composition, students should

- Be aware that it usually takes multiple drafts to create and complete a successful text
- Develop flexible strategies for generating, revising, editing, and proof-reading
- Understand writing as an open process that permits writers to use later invention and re-thinking to revise their work
- Understand the collaborative and social aspects of writing processes
- Learn to critique their own and others' works
- Learn to balance the advantages of relying on others with the responsibility of doing their part
- Use a variety of technologies to address a range of audiences

Faculty in all programs and departments can build on this preparation by helping students learn

- To build final results in stages
- To review work-in-progress in collaborative peer groups for purposes other than editing
- To save extensive editing for later parts of the writing process
- To apply the technologies commonly used to research and communicate within their fields

Knowledge of Conventions

By the end of first-year composition, students should
- Learn common formats for different kinds of texts
- Develop knowledge of genre conventions ranging from structure and paragraphing to tone and mechanics
- Practice appropriate means of documenting their work
- Control such surface features as syntax, grammar, punctuation, and spelling

Faculty in all programs and departments can build on this preparation by helping students learn
- The conventions of usage, specialized vocabulary, format, and documentation in their fields
- Strategies through which better control of conventions can be achieved
[http://www.wpacouncil.org/positions/outcomes.html, accessed 10/17/2008]

Supplements to *A Writer's Resource*

Instructor's Manual (available online in printable format) (www.mhhe.com/awr3)

Deborah Coxwell Teague, Florida State University; Dan Melzer, California State University, Sacramento; Thomas Dinsmore, University of Cincinnati

MLA Quick Reference Guide (ISBN 0-07-730080-7)

Carol Schuck, Ivy Tech Community College
This handy card features the basic guidelines for MLA citation in a convenient, portable format.

APA Quick Reference Guide (ISBN 0-07-730076-9)

Carol Schuck, Ivy Tech Community College
This handy card features the basic guidelines for APA citation in a convenient, portable format.

Partners in Teaching: Instructor Resource Portal for Composition (www.mhhe.com/englishcommunity)

McGraw-Hill is proud to partner with many of the top names in the field to build a *community of teachers helping teachers. Partners in Teaching* features up-to-date scholarly discourse, practical teaching advice, and community support for new and experienced instructors.

The McGraw-Hill Exercise Book (ISBN 0-07-326032-0)

Santi Buscemi, Middlesex College and Susan Popham, University of Memphis
This workbook features numerous sentence-level and paragraph-level editing exercises, as well as exercises in research, documentation, and the writing process.

The McGraw-Hill Exercise Book for Multilingual Writers
(ISBN 0-07-326030-4)
Maggie Sokolik, University of California, Berkeley
This workbook features numerous sentence-level and paragraph-level
editing exercises tailored specifically for multilingual students.

The McGraw-Hill Writer's Journal **(ISBN 0-07-326031-2)**
Lynée Gaillet, Georgia State University
This elegant journal for students includes quotes on writing from famous
authors as well as advice and tips on writing and the writing process.

Dictionary and Vocabulary Resources

McGraw-Hill, in partnership with Merriam Webster, offers a wide variety of language references for students. From the *Collegiate Dictio-
nary* to the *Notebook Thesaurus,* these resources can be packaged with
A Writer's Resource at an affordable price. Please contact your McGraw-
Hill representative directly, email english@mcgraw-hill.com, or call
800-338-3987 for details.

Acknowledgments

When we wrote *A Writer's Resource,* we started with the premise that
it takes a campus to teach a writer. It is also the case that it takes a
community to write a handbook. This text has been a major collaborative effort for all three of us. And over the years, that ever-widen-
ing circle of collaboration has included reviewers, editors, librarians,
faculty colleagues, and family members.

Let us start close to home. Mort Maimon brought to this project his
years of insight and experience as a writer and as a secondary and
post-secondary English teacher. Gillian Maimon, a first-grade teacher,
a PhD candidate, and a writing workshop leader, and Alan Maimon, a
journalist who is expert in using every resource available to writers, inspired and encouraged their mother in this project. Elaine also drew in-
spiration from her young granddaughters, Dasia and Madison Stewart
and Annabelle Elaine Maimon, who already show promise of becom-
ing writers. Rudy Peritz and Lynne Haney reviewed drafts of a number
of chapters, bringing to our cross-curricular mix the pedagogical and
writerly perspectives of, respectively, a law professor and a sociologist.
Jess Peritz, a recent college graduate, was consulted on numerous occasions for her expert advice on making examples both up-to-date and
understandable. David, Genevieve, and Matthew Yancey—whose com-
bined writing experience includes the fields of biology, psychology, med-
icine, computer engineering, mathematics, industrial engineering, and
information technology—helped with examples as well as with their
understandings of writing both inside and outside of the academy.

At Governors State University, Diane Dates Casey, dean of Library Science and Academic Computing, provided research support, while Executive Assistant Penny Purdue was always ready with overall encouragement. At Arizona State University West, Beverly Buddee, executive assistant to the provost, worried with us over this project for many years. Our deepest gratitude goes to Lisa Kammerlocher and Dennis Isbell for the guidelines on critically evaluating Web resources in Chapter 18, as well as to Sharon Wilson. Thanks, too, go to C. J. Jeney and Cheryl Warren for providing assistance. ASU West professors Thomas McGovern and Martin Meznar shared assignments and student papers with us. In the chancellor's office at the University of Alaska Anchorage, Denise Burger, and Christine Tullius showed admirable support and patience.

Several colleagues at Queens College and elsewhere not only shared their insights on teaching and writing, but also gave us valuable classroom materials to use as we saw fit. Our thanks go to Fred Buell, Stuart Cochran, Nancy Comley, Ann Davison, Joan Dupre, Hugh English, Sue Goldhaber, Marci Goodman, Steve Kruger, Eric Lehman, Norman Lewis, Charles Molesworth, Beth Stickney, Amy Tucker, and Stan Walker. We are also grateful to Jane Collins, Jane Hathaway, Jan Tecklin, Christine Timm, Scott Zaluda, Diane Zannoni, and Richard Zeikowitz. The Queens College librarians also gave us help with the researching and documentation chapters, and we thank them, especially Sharon Bonk, Alexandra DeLuise, Izabella Taler, and Manny Sanudo.

We want to give special thanks to the students whose papers we include in full: Ken Tinnes, John Terrell, Rajeev Bector, Matt Shadwell, Esther Hoffman, and Audrey Galeano. We also want to acknowledge the following students who allowed us to use substantial excerpts from their work: Diane Chen, Jennifer Koehler, Ilona Bouzoukashvili, Wilma Ferrarella, Jacob Grossman, and Umawattie Roopnarian.

Our thanks also go to Judy Williamson and Trent Batson for contributing their expertise on writing and computers as well as for sharing what they learned from the Epiphany Project. We are grateful to Harvey Wiener and the late Richard Marius for their permission to draw on their explanations of grammatical points in *The McGraw-Hill Handbook*. We also appreciate the work of Andras Tapolcai and of Charlotte Smith of Adirondack Community College, who collected many of the examples used in the documentation chapters. Maria Zlateva of Boston University, Karen Batchelor of City College of San Francisco, and Daria Ruzicka prepared the ESL materials. Thanks also go to librarians Debora Person, University of Wyoming, and Ronelle K. H. Thompson, Augustana College, who provided us with helpful comments on Tab 5: Researching. Our colleague Don McQuade has inspired us, advised us, and encouraged us throughout the years of this project.

Within the McGraw-Hill organization, many wonderful people have been our true teammates. Tim Julet believed in this project initially and signed us on to what has become a major life commitment. From 1999, Lisa Moore, first as executive editor for the composition list, then as publisher for English, and now as publisher for special projects in Art, Humanities, and Literature, has creatively, expertly, and tirelessly led the group of development editors and in-house experts who have helped us find the appropriate form to bring our insights as composition teachers to the widest possible group of students. We have learned a great deal from Lisa. Thanks also to Christopher Bennem, who had the unenviable job of filling Lisa's shoes as sponsoring editor. Crucial support also came from Beth Mejia, editorial director; David Patterson, publisher for English; and Molly Meneely, market development manager. This book has benefited enormously from three extraordinary development editors: Anne Kemper, development editor; Carla Samodulski, senior development editor; and David Chodoff, senior development editor. All were true collaborators; as the chapters on editing show, the book has benefited enormously from their care and intelligence. Other editorial kudos go out to Meredith Grant, Drew Henry, Karen Herter, Bruce Thaler, Joanna Imm, Judy Voss, Sarah Caldwell, Laura Olson, Elsa Peterson, Aaron Zook, Karen Mauk, Steven Kemper, and Margaret Farley for their tireless work on this project. Thanks as well to Paul Banks, Andrea Pasquarelli, Todd Vaccaro, Alex Rohrs, and Manoj Mehta, without whom there would be no *Catalyst 2.0*. Chanda Feldman and Brett Coker, lead project managers, monitored every detail of production; Cassandra Chu, lead designer, supervised every aspect of the striking text design and cover; and Robin Mouat and Sonia Brown, art editors, were responsible for the stunning visuals that appear throughout the book. Allison Jones, marketing manager and Ray Kelley, Paula Radosevich, Byron Hopkins, Barbara Siry, and Brian Gore, field publishers, have worked tirelessly and enthusiastically to market *A Writer's Resource*. Jeff Brick provided valuable promotional support for the project. We also appreciate the hands-on attention of McGraw-Hill senior executives Mike Ryan, editor-in-chief of the Humanities, Social Sciences, and World Languages group; and Steve Debow, president of the Humanities, Social Sciences, and World Languages group.

Finally, many, many thanks go to the reviewers who read this text, generously shared their perceptions, and had confidence in us as we shaped this book to address the needs of their students. We wish to thank the following instructors:

Content Consultants and Reviewers

Kristina Ambrosia-Conn, Cleveland State University

Frank Ancona, Sussex County Community College

Suzanne Ashby, Pima Community College

James Baskin, Joliet Junior College

Julie Basler, Platt College

Paula Battistelli, Austin Community College

Gary Bays, Wayne College

Nicholas Bekas, Valencia Community College

Michael Benton, Bluegrass Community and Technical College

Paula Berggren, Bernard M. Baruch College

Angela Bilia, University of Akron

Jacqueline Blackwell, Thomas Nelson Community College

Laurel Bollinger, University of Alabama, Huntsville

Eric Branscomb, Salem State College

Tamara Brattoli, Joliet Junior College

Beth Buyserie, Washington State University

Jeffrey Cain, Sacred Heart University

Steve Calatrello, Calhoun Community College

Richard Carr, University of Alaska, Fairbanks

Kathleen J. Cassity, Hawaii Pacific University

Andrew Cavanaugh, University of Maryland

John Chapin, University of Baltimore

Stephanie Clark-Graham, University of Maryland

Joseph Colicchio, Hudson County Community College

Tami Comstock, Arapahoe Community College

Preston Cooper, Austin Community College

Linda Damas, University of Hawaii, Hilo

Mary Ellen Daniloff-Merrill, Southwest Minnesota State University

Michael Day, Northern Illinois University

Rose Day, Central New Mexico Community College

Robert Detmering, Northern Kentucky University

Tom Dow, Moraine Valley Community College

Taylor Emery, Austin Peay State University

Nancy Enright, Seton Hall University

Priscilla Faucette, University of Hawaii, Manoa

Paul J. Ferlazzo, Northern Arizona University

Jason Fichtel, Joliet Junior College

David Fleming, University of Massachusetts–Amherst

Thom Foy, University of Michigan, Dearborn

Lynée Gaillet, Georgia State University

Fernando Ganivett, Florida International University, Miami

Ruth Gerik, University of Texas at Arlington

Mary Val Gerstle, University of Cincinnati

Sam Goldstein, Daytona Beach Community College

Dwonna Goldstone, Austin Peay State University

John Gooch, University of Texas at Dallas

Gary Goodman, University of California, Davis

Nate Gordon, Kishwaukee College

Creed Greer, University of Florida, Gainesville

John Griffiths, Butler County Community College

Lynn Grow, Broward Community College

Elizabeth Grundhoffer, New Mexico State University, Alamogordo

Billie Hara, Texas Christian University

Carolyn Harrison, Oakland Community College, Royal Oak

Kimberly Harrison, Florida International University, Biscayne

Cynthia Haynes, Clemson University

Harold Hellwig, Idaho State University

Bruce Henderson, Fullerton College

Matt Hollrah, University of Central Oklahoma

Dedria A. Humphries, Lansing Community College

Jeffrey Ihlenfeldt, Harrisburg Area Community College, Lancaster

Rebecca Ingalls, Drexell University

Tammy Jabin, Chemeketa Community College

Kim Jacobs-Beck, University of Cincinnati, Clermont College

Doris Jellig, Tidewater Community College

Melanie Jenkins, Snow College

Debra Johanyak, Wayne College

Allen Johnson, Christian Brothers University

Matthew Johnson, Southern Illinois University, Edwardsville

Tracy Johnson, Butte College

Meryl Junious, Kennedy-King College

Judith La Fourest, Ivy Tech Community College, Central Indiana

Jessica Lang, Bernard M. Baruch College

Patricia Lonchar, University of the Incarnate Word

Michael Lynch, Kent State University, Trumbull

Joyce Malek, University of Cincinnati

Tammy Mata, Tarrant County College

Donna Matsumoto, Leeward Community College

Gretchen McCroskey, Northeast State Technical Community College

Jeanne McDonald, Waubonsee Community College

John McDonald, University of Portland

Hildy Miller, Portland State University

Thomas Moretti, University of Maryland

Robin Murray, Eastern Illinois University

Mary Anne Nagler, Oakland Community College

Bev Neiderman, Kent State University

Paul Nolan, Cayuga Community College

Torria Norman, Black Hawk College

Editorial Board of Advisors

Freshman Composition Symposia

Every year McGraw-Hill conducts Freshman Composition Symposia, which are attended by instructors from across the country. These events are an opportunity for editors from McGraw-Hill to gather information about the needs and challenges of instructors teaching the Freshman Composition course. They also offer a forum for the attendees to exchange ideas and experiences with colleagues they might not have otherwise met. The feedback we have received has been invaluable and has contributed—directly or indirectly—to the development of *A Writer's Resource* and its supplements.

Susan Jaye Dauer, Valencia Community College

Michael Day, Northern Illinois University

Rose Day, Central New Mexico Community College

Anne Dearing, Hudson Valley Community College

Michel de Benedictis, Miami-Dade College

Nancy DeJoy, Michigan State University

Christy Desmet, University of Georgia

Brock Dethier, Utah State University

Carlton Downey, Houston Community College

Robert Eddy, Washington State University

Anthony Edgington, University of Toledo

Dan Ferguson, Amarillo College

Bonnie Finkelstein, Montgomery County Community College

Steve Fox, Indiana University–Purdue University, Indianapolis

Sherrin Frances, San Jacinto College, Pasadena

Elaine Fredericksen, University of Texas, El Paso

Karen Gardiner, University of Alabama, Tuscaloosa

Judith Gardner, University of Texas, San Antonio

Elizabeth Gassel, Darton College

Joanna Gibson, Texas A&M University

Lois Gilmore, Bucks County Community College

Chuck Gonzalez, Central Florida Community College, Ocala

John Gooch, University of Texas, Dallas

Cathy Gorvine, Delgado Community College

Frank Gunshanan, Daytona State College

Emily Gwinn, Glendale Community College

Audley Hall, North West Arkansas Community College

Carolyn Handa, University of Alabama, Tuscaloosa

Rebecca Heintz, Polk Community College

Dedria Humphries, Lansing Community College

Kim Jameson, Oklahoma City Community College

Nanette Jaynes, Wesleyan College

Theodore Johnston, El Paso Community College

Peggy Jolly, University of Alabama, Birmingham

Joseph Jones, University of Memphis

Rebecca Kajs, Anne Arundel Community College

Pam Kannady, Tulsa Community College

Shelley Kelly, College of Southern Nevada

Elizabeth Kessler, University of Houston

Kirk Kidwell, Michigan State University

Roxanne Kirkwood, Marshall University

Sandra Lakey, Pennsylvania College of Technology

William Lennertz, Santiago Canyon College

Tom Lovin, Southwestern Illinois College

Heidi Marshall, Florida Community College

Denise Martone, New York University

Barry Mauer, University of Central Florida

Michael McCready, University of Mississippi

Sharon McGee, Southern Illinois University, Edwardsville

Janice McIntire-Strasburg, St. Louis University

Patrick McLaughlin, Lakeland Community College

Shellie Michael, Volunteer State Community College

John Miles, University of New Mexico

Susan Miller, Santa Fe Community College

Susan Miller-Cochran, North Carolina State University, Raleigh

Jennifer Nelson, College of Southern Nevada

Donna Nelson-Beene, Bowling Green State University

Lindee Owens, University of Central Florida

Matthew Parfitt, Boston University

Irvin Peckham, Louisiana State University

Chere Peguesse, Valdosta State University

Bruce Peppard, El Camino College

Rich Peraud, St. Louis Community College, Meramec

David Peterson, University of Nebraska, Omaha

Helen Frances Poehlman, Blinn College

Susan Popham, University of Memphis

Mara Rainwater, Keiser University

Christa Raney, University of North Alabama

Beverly Reed, College of Dupage

Patricia Reid, University of Toledo

David Reinheimer, Southeast Missouri State University

Mandi Riley, Florida A&M University

Dixil Rodriguez, Tarrant County College

Denise Rogers, University of Louisiana

Lou Ethel Rolliston, Bergen Community College

Shirley Rose, Purdue University

Kathleen Ryan, University of Montana

Mary Sauer, Indiana University–Purdue University, Indianapolis

Mark Saunders, Front Range Community College

Matthew Schmeer, Johnson County Community College

Jane Schreck, Bismark State College

Carol Schuck, Ivy Tech Community College

Marc Scott, New Mexico State University

Susan Sebok, South Suburban College

Wendy Sharer, East Carolina University

E. Stone Shiflet, Capella University

Patrick Slattery, University of Arkansas

Beverly Slaughter, Brevard Community College, Melbourne

James Sodon, St. Louis Community College, Florissant Valley

Ann Spurlock, Mississippi State University

Wayne Stein, University of Central Oklahoma

Kip Strasma, Illinois Central College

Beverly Stroud, Greenville Technical College

Paul Tanner, Utah Valley University

Todd Taylor, University of North Carolina

William Thelin, University of Akron

Gordon Thomas, University of Idaho

Donna Thomsen, Johnson & Wales University

Martha Tolleson, Collin College

Pauline Uchmanowicz, State University of New York, New Paltz

Frank Vaughn, Campbell University

Stephanie Venza, Brookhaven College

Philip Virgen, Wilbur Wright College

Judy Welch, Miami-Dade College

Christina Wells, Northern Virginia Community College

Jeff Wiemelt, Southeastern Louisiana University

John Ziebell, College of Southern Nevada

Supplements Team

Preston Allen, Miami-Dade College

Santi Buscemi, Middlesex College

Deborah Coxwell Teague, Florida State University

Thomas Dinsmore, University of Cincinnati, Clermont College

Lynée Gaillet, Georgia State University

Dan Melzer, California State University, Sacramento

Susan Popham, University of Memphis

Lynette Reini-Grandell, Normandale Community College

Carol Schuck, Ivy Tech Community College

Maggie Sokolik, University of California, Berkeley

Technology Consultants

Cheryl Ball, Illinois State University

Dene Grigar, Washington State University

Elizabeth Nist, Anoka-Ramsey Community College

Donna Reiss, Tidewater Community College

Rich Rice, Texas Tech University

Heather Robinson, City University of New York, York College

James Sodon, St. Louis Community College, Florissant Valley

ESL Consultants

Karen Batchelor, City College of San Francisco

Cherry Campbell, University of California, Los Angeles

Christine T. Francisco, City College of San Francisco

Candace A. Henry, Westmoreland Community College

Maria Zlateva, Boston University

Design and Cover Reviewers

Kristina Ambrosia-Conn, Cleveland State University

Francesco Ancona, Sussex County Community College

Allison Arnold, University of New Orleans

Suzanne Ashby, Pima Community College

James Baskin, Joliet Junior College

Paula Berggren, Baruch College

Tamara Brattoli, Joliet Junior College

Jeffrey Cain, Sacred Heart University

Steve Calatrello, Calhoun Community College

Thom Foy, University of Michigan, Dearborn

Lynée Gaillet, Georgia State University

Fernando Ganivet, Florida International University
John Gooch, University of Texas, Dallas
Gary Goodman, University of California, Davis
Jay Gordon, Youngstown State University
Michael Grimm, Linn-Benton Community College
Billie Hara, Texas Christian University
Kimberly Harrison, Florida International University
Bruce Henderson, Fullerton College
Matt Hollrah, University of Central Oklahoma
Kim Jacobs-Beck, University of Cincinnati, Clermont College

Allen Johnson, Christian Brothers University
Tracy Johnson, Butte College
Judith La Fourest, Ivy Tech Community College
Jessica Lang, Baruch College
Patricia Lonchar, University of the Incarnate Word
Tammy Mata, Tarrant County College
Donna Matsumoto, Leeward Community College
Hildy Miller, Portland State University
Mary Anne Nagler, Oakland Community College
Bev Neiderman, Kent State University

Marguerite Newcomb, University of Texas, San Antonio
Christa Raney, University of North Alabama
Barbara Rico, Loyola Marymount University
Heather Robinson, City University of New York, York College
Robert Royar, Morehead State University
David Salomon, Russell Sage College
Mary Seel, Broome Community College
Kathleen White, Pima Community College
Anita Wyman, Hillsborough Community College

Focus Group and Seminar Participants

Joyce Adams, Brigham Young University
Jeannette Adkins, Tarrant County Community College
Jim Allen, College of Dupage
Sonja Andrus, Collin College
Marcy Bauman, Lansing Community College
Sue Beebe, Texas State University, San Marcos
Candace Bergstrom, Houston Community College
Bruce Bogdon, Houston Community College
Barbara Bonallo, Miami-Dade College
Sarah Bruton, Fayetteville Tech Community College
Joe Bryan, El Paso Community College
Alma Bryant, University of South Florida
Lauryn Angel Cann, Collin College
Diane Carr, Midlands Technical College
Lucia Cherciu, Dutchess Community College
Regina Clemens Fox, Arizona State University

Terry Cole, Laguardia Community College
Keith Comer, University of Canterbury
Genevieve Coogan, Houston Community College
Dagmar Corrigan, University of Houston
Marla DeSoto, Glendale Community College
Debra Dew, University of Colorado, Colorado Springs
Erika Dieters, Moraine Valley Community College
Michael Donnelly, Ball State University
Marilyn Douglas-Jones, Houston Community College
Carlton Downey, Houston Community College
Lisa Dresdner, Norwalk Community College
Heather Eaton, Daytona State College
George Edwards, Tarrant County Community College
Richard Enos, Texas Christian University
Nancy Enright, Seton Hall University

Paula Eschliman, Richland College
Karin Evans, College of DuPage
Jennie Fauls, Columbia College–Chicago
Africa Fine, Florida Atlantic University
Stacha Floyd, Wayne County Community College
John Freeman, El Paso Community College
Casey Furlong, Glendale Community College
Karen Gardiner, University of Alabama, Tuscaloosa
Mary Lee Geary, Front Range Community College
Ruth Gerik, University of Texas, Arlington
Phyllis Gooden, Atlantic International University, Chicago
Jay Gordon, Youngstown State University
Lisa Gordon, Columbus State Community College
Steffen Guenzel, University of Alabama, Tuscaloosa
John Hagerty, Auburn University

Jonathan Hall, Rutgers University, Newark

Dustin Hanvey, Pasadena Area Community College

Bryant Hayes, Bernard M. Baruch College

Shawn Hellman, Pima Community College

Maren Henry, University of West Georgia

Kevin Hicks, Alabama State University

Brandy James, University of West Georgia

Peggy Jolly, University of Alabama, Birmingham

Nicole Khoury, Arizona State University

Jessica Kidd, University of Alabama, Tuscaloosa

Lindsay Lewan, Arapahoe Community College

Victoria Lisle, Auburn University

Colleen Lloyd, Cuyahoga Community College

Margaret Lowry, University of Texas, Arlington

Andrew Manno, Raritan Valley Community College

Shirley McBride, Collin College

Dan Melzer, California State University, Sacramento

Erica Messenger, Bowling Green State University

Joyce Miller, Collin College

Dorothy Minor, Tulsa Community College

Webster Newbold, Ball State University

Gordon O'Neal, Collin College

Maryann Perlman, Wayne County Community College

Joann Pinkston-McDuffie, Daytona State College

Deborah Prickett, Jacksonville State University

Roberta Proctor, Palm Beach Community College, Lake Worth

Helen Raica-Klotz, Saginaw Valley State University

Sharon Roberts, Auburn University

Cassanda Robison, Central Florida Community College

Michael Ronan, Houston Community College

Jane Rosencrans, J. S. Reynolds Community College

Mark Saunders, Front Range Community College

Mary Beth Schillacci, Houston Community College

Shelita Shaw, Moraine Valley Community College

Jenny Sheppard, New Mexico State University

Michelle Sidler, Auburn University

Jean Sorensen, Grayson County College

Cathy Stablein, College of Dupage

Wayne Stein, University of Central Oklahoma

Martha Tolleson, Collin College

Saundra Towns, Bernard M. Baruch College

George Trail, University of Houston

Bryon Turman, North Carolina A&T University

Christopher Twiggs, Florida Community College

Kathryn Valentine, New Mexico State University

Kevin Waltman, University of Alabama, Tuscaloosa

Maryann Whitaker, University of Alabama, Tuscaloosa

Joseph White, Fayetteville Tech Community College

Virginia Wicher, Tarrant County Community College

Reginald Williams, Daytona State College

Elizabeth Woodworth, Auburn University, Montgomery

Elaine P. Maimon

Janice H. Peritz

Kathleen Blake Yancey

About the Authors

Elaine P. Maimon is president of Governors State University in the south suburbs of Chicago, where she is also Professor of English. Previously she was chancellor of the University of Alaska Anchorage, provost (chief campus officer) at Arizona State University West, and Vice President of Arizona State University as a whole. In the 1970s, she initiated and then directed the Beaver College writing-across-the-curriculum program, one of the first WAC programs in the nation. A founding executive board member of the National Council of Writing Program Administrators (WPA), she has directed national institutes to improve the teaching of writing and to disseminate the principles of writing across the curriculum. With a PhD in English from the University of Pennsylvania, where she later helped to create the Writing Across the University (WATU) program, she has also taught and served as an academic administrator at Haverford College, Brown University, and Queens College.

Janice Haney Peritz is an associate professor of English who has taught college writing for more than thirty years, first at Stanford University, where she received her PhD in 1978, and then at the University of Texas at Austin; Beaver College; and Queens College, City University of New York. From 1989 to 2002, she directed the Composition Program at Queens College, where in 1996, she also initiated the college's writing-across-the-curriculum program and the English department's involvement with the Epiphany Project and cyber-composition. She also worked with a group of CUNY colleagues to develop The Write Site, an online learning center, and more recently directed the CUNY Honors College at Queens College for three years. Currently, she is back in the English department doing what she loves most: full-time classroom teaching of writing, literature, and culture.

Kathleen Blake Yancey is the Kellogg W. Hunt Professor of English and director of the Graduate Program in Rhetoric and Composition at Florida State University. Past president of the Council of Writing Program Administrators (WPA) and past chair of the Conference on College Composition and Communication (CCCC), she is president of the National Council of Teachers of English (NCTE). In addition, she co-directs the Inter/National Coalition on Electronic Portfolio Research. She has directed several institutes focused on electronic portfolios and on service learning and reflection, and with her colleagues in English education, she is working on developing a program in new literacies. Previously, she has taught at UNC Charlotte and at Clemson University, where she directed the Pearce Center for Professional Communication and created the Class of 1941 Studio for Student Communication, both of which are dedicated to supporting communication across the curriculum.